The Laws of Relationship

37 Unexpendable Truths about Relationship that will Change Your Life Forever

ERIC O. ENEJOH

WESTBOW
PRESS®
A DIVISION OF THOMAS NELSON
& ZONDERVAN

Copyright © 2019 Eric O. Enejoh.

All rights reserved. No part of this book may be used or reproduced by any means, graphic, electronic, or mechanical, including photocopying, recording, taping or by any information storage retrieval system without the written permission of the author except in the case of brief quotations embodied in critical articles and reviews.

This book is a work of non-fiction. Unless otherwise noted, the author and the publisher make no explicit guarantees as to the accuracy of the information contained in this book and in some cases, names of people and places have been altered to protect their privacy.

WestBow Press books may be ordered through booksellers or by contacting:

WestBow Press
A Division of Thomas Nelson & Zondervan
1663 Liberty Drive
Bloomington, IN 47403
www.westbowpress.com
1 (866) 928-1240

Because of the dynamic nature of the Internet, any web addresses or links contained in this book may have changed since publication and may no longer be valid. The views expressed in this work are solely those of the author and do not necessarily reflect the views of the publisher, and the publisher hereby disclaims any responsibility for them.

Any people depicted in stock imagery provided by Getty Images are models, and such images are being used for illustrative purposes only. Certain stock imagery © Getty Images.

Scripture quotations marked GW are taken from GOD'S WORD®, © 1995 God's Word to the Nations. Used by permission of Baker Publishing Group.

Scripture quotations marked KJV are taken from the King James Bible.

ISBN: 978-1-9736-4716-4 (sc)
ISBN: 978-1-9736-4717-1 (e)

Print information available on the last page.

WestBow Press rev. date: 2/11/2019

Dedication

This book is dedicated to my lovely daughter, Praise Eric Enejoh, whose emergence adds beauty to my world.

Contents

Acknowledgment ix
Forward x
Introduction xi

1 The Law of Proximity 1
2 The Law of Dedication 4
3 The Law of Common Language 6
4 The Law of Clarity 8
5 The Law of Common Goals 10
6 The Law of the "Life Goal" 13
7 The Law of Sacrifice 16
8 The Law of Responsibility 18
9 The Law of the Pillar 20
10 Law of Mutual Consent 22
11 The Law of Ignition 24
12 The Law of Like Feather 26
13 The Law of Natural Effect 29
14 The Law of Stability 31
15 The Law of The Rough Road 33
16 The Law of Symbiosis 35
17 The Law of Relative Balance 38
18 The Law of the Coloured Glass 42
19 The Law of Influence 44
20 The Law of Investment 47
21 The Law of Authority 51
22 The Law of Identity 53
23 The Law of Flexibility 55

24	The Law of Sanity	58
25	The Law of Intimacy	60
26	The Law of the Open Door	62
27	The Law of Reconciliation	65
28	The Law of Persistence	67
29	The Law of Affinity Between Opposite Sexes	70
30	The Law of Emergency	72
31	The Law of the Boundary	74
32	The Law of Perpetuity	78
33	The Law of Integrity	81
34	The Law of Legacy	84
35	The Law of Dignity	87
36	The Law of Compatibility	89
37	The Law of Consistency	95
38	Operating and Suspending Natural Laws	97
39	Remember the Golden Rule	100

Acknowledgment

My most sincere and profound appreciation goes to the Most High God for giving me the inspiration for this work.

I like to appreciate my wife, Favour, for her love, encouragement and strong support to me in ministry.

I, also, wish to appreciate my great friends in the RCCG FCT Province 7 Prayer Champion Department, Emmanuel Idu, Gabriel Nimmak and Bode Adebola, who are very supportive in the course of my work on this book.

I cannot fail to mention members of staff of KHMS Jahi Abuja, who created enthralling relationship environment. Thank you!

I like to say a big thank you to my mentor, Pastor Ededet Otu-Bassey, whose love and support has become one of God's sustaining pillars in my work and ministry.

I like to specially appreciate Jennifer Ajukwu and Joy Chia who invested time to straighten some of the ideas in this book.

I, also, appreciate all my numerous friends in church, home and other places, pardon me if I do not mention your name here, but you are very wonderful and looking at my relationship with you, I have come to understand that in relationship one must be guided.

Forward

Laws are principles and regulations which have been established to guide or guard people or the doing of a thing. We find that laws are targeted to influence the life of a people and that seem to be the cardinal achievement of any good law. All laws derive from God drawn mostly from the sensibility of mankind.

The author of "The Laws of Relationship" has adopted in his book this basic cardinal for influencing the reader; by helping the realization of the need to live within God's ordained life principles. Laws regulate and act as a guard and guide and these principles have been broken down here in the most appreciable way, in this book.

This book is written in a very unique way and in the most simplistic format that makes reading easy also makes comprehension very easy too. Life principles are broken down for the ease of practice and should make the readership accept it as a practical guide to a good and rewarding life to the individual reader in particular and the public in general.

It is a must read for everyone mindful to live a God pleasing life as we do not live life alone at any point in time. In the book the Questions for Reflection systematically arranged following every topic will be useful guide and help to drive the understanding deeper: practice it!

I encourage you beyond reading the book to retain it as a guide and a regular check; and as a monitor in all our work while on the surface of this earth. It is a book quite revealing, interesting and suitable as everyday guide. It is as good for the old as it is for the young men and young women whose life we owe God to help to form. Read it and keep it close always.

Ameh Franklyn Adejo.
Legal Practitioner & Pastor in Charge of Area

Introduction

Life is all about relationship.

We are surrounded by people. Our happiness and effectiveness depend on how well we get along with them. We work with our head but relate with our heart. We may lose effectiveness when our heart is troubled as a result of friction or strife with people.

The fear of pain associated with relating with people and how it affects our work, has caused many to shut the door to their heart, hoping they can get on with their lives without being affected. They starve themselves of true happiness that comes with heartfelt relationships and the joy only love brings; denying themselves the opportunity to build quality relationships and store up beautiful memories.

When you open your heart to people, this challenges them to reciprocate. When you understand how to relate with people, they will be ready to go to the ends of the earth for you, not minding the cost.

We all have reasons why we relate with people. The following, to a large extent, are true about relationship:

- Our happiness depends on how well we can relate with our friends and families.
- Our joy depends on how sincere we are when we share our time and resources with others.
- Our effectiveness depends on how well we get along with sub-ordinates, colleagues and boss.
- Our character is influenced or tailored by how well we understand the people around us and handle conflicts.

Therefore, our daily lives, effectiveness, health, happiness and joy, to a large extent, centre around relationship.

Arguably, the primary objective of education is to make you better in relating with people. If you lack basic relationship skills, you are not schooled.

I have written this book to challenge and build you into personality capable of sustaining quality relationships, and also, to give you tangible ingredients that will ultimately make you a better person. This book brings to your hands laws that guide relationships, thoroughly explained for easy assimilation, and laws that will become our lifestyle.

I charge you, read diligently every line, paragraph and page. Testimonies await you in Jesus Name (Amen).

1
The Law of Proximity

Closeness and availability increase fondness.

Falacy	Absence makes the heart grow fonder.
Fact	We tend to love those who are close and available to help us when we need them the most, not necessarily the best people in the world.
Basic Truth	It is true that not every body is a hopeless romantic, but if you love or value a person, the only way you can show it is if the person is close by. Distance is one of the constraint to building love and respect. If you are not able to push past the barrier of distance and invest time in those you love, your love has little or nothing to offer. When it comes to increasing fondness, do not say it; just make effort to be as close as possible. Actions enhancing proximity can light the fire of affection in anyone. You cannot light the fire of affection in a person, if you maintain great distance from him or her.

Most people erroneously believe that this law only applies to people who are trying to initiate a relationship. The law has stronger effect on a well-established relationship than the one that is yet to begin. If a married man, for instance, leaves home early and maintains late nights, he will get home one day and discover that his wife and children are all gone. Similarly, if a woman keeps too much distance from her spouse, it is very likely that another woman will take her place. Proximity does not only ignite the fire of affection, but also determines it sustenance.

Required

Push past the barrier of distance; close gaps between you and the people you love, this will reveal your heartfelt intentions towards them.

Questions for Reflection

1. What three (3) things have created relationship gap between you and those you value/love. (The people you value may include your colleague in the office, church members, your associates, friends and family relations) You may list more than three.

   a. ....
   b. ....
   c. ....

2. List three (3) practical steps you can take to remove these barriers. (Your action step may include: regular visit, paying of a

colleague's child school fees; spending more time with those I value; taking a walk once a week/month with those I value, etc.)

a. ....
b. ....
c. ....

2

The Law of Dedication

Concentration improves quality.

Falacy	Familiarity breeds contempt.
Fact	It is not the quantity of time we spend with those we love that matters but the quality. Let your commitment to expressing your love to your loved ones, be profound.
Basic Truth	When we choose to spend time with people, we must think of all the ways to make the moments memorable and time together remarkable. Prepare the gift to give, the words to say and the ways to lift the persons' spirit. These things have lasting effect on people and make them willing to see us again.
Required	When you are with those you love, give them your undivided attention.

Question for Reflection

1. Mention five (5) things you can do to make the time you spend with people memorable.

   a. ....
   b. ....
   c. ....
   d. ....
   e. ....

3

The Law of Common Language

Consistent mutual understanding brings growth.

Falacy	Good relationship involves people naturally speaking the same language.
Fact	The world is made up of people from different walks of life and tribes, with different personal experiences and innate abilities—no two people are the same. To interact effectively with other people, we must make conscious efforts to understand them.
Basic Truth	In close relationship, we do not just communicate, we relate. People must understand each other in any kind of profitable relationship, if the relationship is to stand the test of time. In the real sense, they must speak the same language. They must be ready to lend helping hand, caring, loving and appreciative. These elements make people to be willing to read and understand you, and when you make positive moves, they make moves to meet you there. The law of the common language comes into play when these elements are present. When

they are absent, people only play along, they don't relate.

People may be excellent communicators, yet lack the ability to speak the same language with those they truly value or love. If you cannot speak the same language as another, you cannot keep that person close to you, for a long time. You cannot enjoy the company of people with whom you cannot relate with a common language.

Required

Relationship has its own language. To enjoy relationship with people you must strive to speak a common language with them.

Questions for Reflection

1. Mention three (3) ways you can improve your relationship with people by communicating at their frequency. (Your answer may include: identify with their loses; know their weaknesses; render helping hands; give advice on ways to solve their problems)

    a. ....
    b. ....
    c. ....

2. What three (3) things can you do to help people who value you communicate at your frequency. (Your answer may include: tell them my personal history; tell them about my likes and dislikes; tell them my best and worst experiences; be patient with them)

    a. ....
    b. ....
    c. ....

4
The Law of Clarity

Communication is the fuel of relationship.

Falacy	I can get along fine without much communication.
Fact	Poor communication starves relationship.
Basic Truth	A relationship is as good as the communication between the parties involved. People often take this fact for granted in their interactions with others. Most times, leaders communicate without clarity leaving followers to their assumptions and expect result at the end of the day, only to be disappointed.

Good communicators ensure clarity. When they communicate, they are precise and leave no room to ambiguity. They say what they mean and they mean what they say. When you fail to be clear, you are preparing yourself for conflict, whether you like it or not.

Communication is a two way traffic; you must seek to understand first, to be understood. You have to show patience when interacting with people; so that it will be easy for

> **Required**

them to express their feelings and opinions, also correct them with love and respect where necessary—criticize constructively.

Whenever you communicate, seek to be clear, precise and listen for feedback.

Questions for Reflection

1. What five (5) things must you have at the back of your mind to communicate most effectively? (Your answer may include: say exactly what I mean; mean what I say; I will not interrupt people when they are still talking; I will not be judgmental; I will make effort to understand what a person is trying to tell me before I respond, etc.)

   a. ....
   b. ....
   c. ....
   d. ....
   e. ....

5

The Law of Common Goals

Common goals give value to relationship.

Falacy	Relationship is necessary simply to have somebody to talk to.
Fact	"Two are better than one; because they have a good reward for their labour. For if they fall, the one will lift his fellow: but woe to him that is alone when he falleth; for he hath not another to help him up" (Eccleciastes 4:9 – 10, King James Version).
Basic Truth	Relationship draw strength from common goals which people must consciously seek to achieve. Two of the most common goals in relationship are joy (or happiness) and getting help in times of need. People do not always go into relationship knowing exactly what they want from it, but when relationship cannot make them happy, they simply want to cut off. However, if you make up your mind to make other people happy, you will find happiness in most of relationship you engage in, and

be positioned to break off any relationship you think is toxic.

We cannot do everything by ourselves and even the things we can do for ourselves, we sometimes are unable to. Many times we have shortage of time, money, materials and physical strength. If we do not get help when we need it, it may appear the world is coming to an end; especially, when the people we consider to be our friends and families are not willing to help. It is, therefore, important that we make it our goals, to make people around us happy, be ready to render help when the need arises and to avoid emotional attachment with people who are not willing to reciprocate.

Required

To give value to your relationship, give it goals to achieve.

Questions for Reflection

1. List five (5) goals you want your relationship with your spouse to achieve.

    a. ....
    b. ....
    c. ....
    d. ....
    e. ....

2. List five (5) goals you want your relationship with other people to achieve.

   a. ....
   b. ....
   c. ....
   d. ....
   e. ....

Some people's life goals are shallow. Picture a man whose life goal is to always have clothes for Christmas. If he is broke in December, he may go and borrow money, or even steal, just to have Christmas clothes. Without any concern for the injury he inflicts on the people who care about him. This is the problem with shallow life goals; the costly price we have to pay for something so small. If your life goal is small, you may give up the relationship you cherish for a plate of porridge or a piece of silver.

No life goal is bigger than quality relationship with good people. The truth is a solid relationship is worth more than gold. Bishop David Abioye tailored his life goal around Bishop David Oyedepo, the founder of Living Faith Church Comission. He stood by him all through the tough times until the ministry became a huge success. Pastor Enoch A. Adeboye of the Redeemed Christian Church of God, expanded the vision of the founder, Reverend Akindayomi, even after the founder was long gone. Bishop David Oyedepo and Reverend Akindayomi understood the secret – a quality relationship with good people is worth more than gold. Building a solid relationship for a lasting legacy became their life goals.

Required

Whatever you want to achieve in life, make it one of your life goals to seek out good people and build quality relationship with them. Whatever you achieve in life is secondary to the relationship you keep. Good relationship is good business.

6

The Law of the "Life Goal"

A man's biggest desire defines his relationship.

Falacy	People can relate without any concern for their personal desires.
Fact	People's life goals influence the kind of people they seek out for relationship and the relationship they maintain.
Basic Truth	People's life goals are their biggest singular desires. They cannot sacrifice them on the alter of relationship; life goals serve as the basis for their relationship. When people discover that a relationship has not met their life goals, they immediately seek out another relationship that can. If a person's life goal is to acquire a lot of money for the sake of having money and the pride it brings, he can do almost anything to acquire that money. For instance, Judas betrayed Jesus for money and Gehazi betrayed his master's trust for some pieces of silver. The end of both Judas and Gehazi were, however, disastrous. When your life goal has no objective of adding value to people you are heading for destruction.

Question for Reflection

1. Mention three (3) ways you can always relate with people so that they will be willing and able to help you achieve your biggest goals in life. (Your answers may include: Spending more time with people who are of great value to me in order to understand them better; Solving the problems of those who work for me; Making my vision beneficial to people who are ready to be part of my success)

   a. ....
   b. ....
   c. ....

7

The Law of Sacrifice

Sacrifice is the required price for improving relationship.

Falacy	A good relationship is cheap.
Fact	The degree of sacrifice defines the quality of love. Unwillingness to make sacrifice result to lack of interest or love.
Basic Truth	There is no relationship without sacrifice. Infact, it takes a great deal of sacrifice to maintain close ties.

The prodigal son was tired of making sacrifices, so he demanded for his inheritance and it was given to him. After which he went to a far away country, where he squandered everything he had. Seeing that he had nothing left, and with no where to go, he chose to return home. In the light of his actions, he believed he had lost his place and begged his father to accept him as one of his servants.

In a relationship, when we do not make the appropriate sacrifice as at when due, we relinguish our rights.

> **Required**
>
> To build and sustain relationship you must ascertain the required sacrifice per time and respond appropriately.

Questions for Reflection

1. What are the prices you are willing to pay to improve your relationship with those you value? (Mention the first five (5) that comes to mind)

    a. ....
    b. ....
    c. ....
    d. ....
    e. ....

8

The Law of Responsibility

Responsibility gives staminer to relationship.

Falacy — People who love you, will continue to love you whether you behave responsibly or not.

Fact — No man will do everything for you.

Basic Truth — You must take responsibility for relationship. If your relationship is to stand the test of time, you must be consistent in playing your part and showing appreciation. It is bad and irresponsible to neglect your responsibilities, while you watch your partner shoulder all responsibilities. It is a gross irresponsibility, to allow your partner in a relationship to do everything.

People will not continue to shoulder all responsibilities to sustain a relationship without their partner's support. All parties must be able to pull their weight in being supportive of one another for the relationship to work. Anything short of this, will lead to the dearth of the relationship.

Relationship is like fire, being irresponsible

> **Required**

is taking out one of the elements that keeps it burning.

It is your responsibility to seek out your role and make tangible input to keep relationship going and mutually beneficial.

Questions for Reflection

Please check.

1. Do you take responsibilities for your lack of performance or blame others?

    ❏ I take responsibility for my shortfalls and lack of performance
    ❏ I blame my inadequacies on people close to me

2. How prompt are you in returning calls?

    ❏ Very prompt   ❏ Not Prompt

3. How often do you deliver on your promises?

    ❏ Always   ❏ Seldom

4. Who pay the bills in your relationships?

    ❏ Paying the bills is always a joint responsibility
    ❏ I take responsibility for paying the bills
    ❏ Others pay the bills for me

If any of your answers is anything other than "i", you need to step up and start taking responsibility to give your relationship stamina.

9

The Law of the Pillar

One person always loves more.

Falacy	People have equal ability to love.
Fact	Everyone is capable of love, but some more than others.
Basic Truth	Our ability to love differs, but we all can love most sincerely (from our heart). We can love and be loved in return.

Those who love more are the pillars of the relationship, while those on the receiving end are the dependants. The pillars are love givers, while the dependants are love seekers. The pillars often find love wherever they go, simply because they love freely; but the dependants feel unloved until they find pillars.

The pillars are the burden bearers in relationship. They do everything in their power to keep the relationship going. Once a pillar is tired of a relationship, the relationship is through.

While two pillars can be very intimate, two dependants cannot maintain intimate relationship. However, the dependant can feel fulfilled when with a pillar. If you are the pillar in any relationship do not feel terrible as long as the other party is not making effort to make a mess of your feelings. But if you are the dependant, make the pillar know, by your appreciative action, that you care and you will always be there.

Required

If you cannot equal your partner in showing love, you must match him in reciprocating love.

Questions for Reflection

1. Mention three (3) things you can do to prove to others that you love them. (Your answer may include: be the first to make a call when you care about a person, teach a person to give by giving quality gift, always be ready to forgive when the one you love offends you)

   a. ....
   b. ....
   c. ....

2. Mention three (3) ways to reciprocate love. (Your answer may include: be quick to return calls; saying thank you in a special way – may be, by giving gifts; avoid careless words which make people feel cheap for loving you)

   a. ....
   b. ....
   c. ....

10

Law of Mutual Consent

There is no relationship without a mutual consent.

Falacy

You can bully people to stay loyal to you as long as you have a special advantage over them.

Fact

You can buy a hand but not a heart. Loyalty is optional.

Basic Truth

You cannot make people your friends if they are not willing to be. No matter how much you love a person, it is the person's prerogative to choose to walk by you. You do not have such power to make someone your friend against his will.

No amount of money can buy a man's heart. However, when people see your sincerity and patience, they may get to like you and open their hearts to you. You must give the people you love, the time to consider if they want to love you in return or not.

For instance, when it comes to choosing a spouse, you must be sincere with yourself. You should not marry someone who does not truly care about you. Give the person you love the chance to prove if they want the same with you, otherwise your marriage will end on paper. The same is true about a loyal follower or a friend. If a person does not want you, give him space and lighten your emotional burden.

Required

To be sure about where you stand with people in your life, give them the chance to be sure they want you around them.

Question for Reflection

1. Mention three (3) things you can always do to gain or sustain the loyalty of those you value. (Your answer may include; empathies with them when they have a bad experience; share their joy when they have a major breakthrough; always find a way to help people solve their problems)

   a. ....
   b. ....
   c. ....

11

The Law of Ignition

Great courage and tact are required to make people like what we have to offer.

Falacy — Every good relationship starts by accident.

Fact — You must have the courage to present what you have, stand and listen, read the other party and strive to appeal to the party's emotion or reasoning. You must say what the person likes to hear and not what you feel like saying. You must do what the person wants you to do in the manner he wants it, not what you want or the way you want it.

Basic Truth — If the ignition process is very successful the relationship gets a smooth take off and possibly ride, as though the people have known each other for a long time. If the ignition process is not very successful, the people may struggle and continue to make amends until they settle in the course of the relationship. If it fails completely, people may detest each other and may even become enemies.

More so, the ignition process may be

Required

successful but the person(s) that initiated the relationship might have paid a price too high that they may not deliver on their promises or meet expectations in the course of the relationship. It is, therefore, left to the second party to cover up or give up.

When the ignition process fails, you have two options: the first is to invest time, money or other resources to motivate the other party, and the second is simply seek out other people available and willing.

To initiate a relationship, read the other party and count the cost before you take a leap. Patience and tact are, therefore, required for ignition.

Question for Reflection

1. List five (5) factors you consider before going into any relationship—be it business, platonic or love relationship. (Your answer may include; level of exposure; educational level; differences in personal history, including past successes and failure; differences in culture; differences in religion, etc.)

   a. ....
   b. ....
   c. ....
   d. ....
   e. ....

These factors may not stop you from relating but they will guide you in the manner in which you approach the other party or in the manner of your self-comporting and enhance your acceptability.

12

The Law of Like Feather

To sustain relationship with a person, the person must become like you or you must become like the person.

Falacy — You can be intimate with people without being influenced by them.

Fact — People often get along on grounds that they are alike—Birds of same feathers flocks together.

Basic Truth — People will observe you from a distance but will not relate until they realize that they share several things in common with you. We are comfortable around people who are like us in many ways. When there are too many differences between a person and another, closeness will be virtually impossible between them. To relate with someone who value relationship, relate as family; to relate with someone who is generous, relate as a giver; to relate with an orphan, relate as someone who is all too familiar with grief and loss; to encourage someone who has trust issues, relate as someone whose trust has been betrayed but not afraid to take the risk to trust and love people. We relate with people on the grounds on which we are alike.

For us to be a part of a group we value or be with the people we love, we may need to change or act differently. We must show the aspect of us that looks like the ones we value and work on strenghtening positive values that are alike. After which we can walk along, give up alittle of ourselves and become more like them; they will give up alittle of themselves and pick up alittle of ours. Little by little we become more and more alike, thereby enhancing better understanding of each other.

Required

To maintain closeness to those you value or love, relate on grounds on which you are alike.

Question for Reflection

1. Mention three (3) instances when you have had problems with someone whose relationship you value, because you could not find a common ground with that person.

   a. ....
   b. ....
   c. ....

2. List three (3) ways you could have related differently to have ensured a smoother relationship. (Your answer may include; being more patient with him or her; do not make reference to past issues of differences when things go wrong; seek to understand

his or her point of view, and then take him or her on a journey to your point of view, etc.)

a. ....
b. ....
c. ....

13

The Law of Natural Effect

The hard way is not always the only way.

Falacy	If it is not difficult, it is not worth it.
Fact	There are people God has positioned to love us for who we are. All we need do is to reciprocate. The more of such people we are able to keep around us, the less difficult life will be for us.
Basic Truth	When it comes to true love, the hard way is not the only way, and more often, the hard is not the way at all. Most people often experience heart breaks because they set their heart on loving people who do not even know they exist. Only people who love you, will give you the emotional support required to create a suitable psychological environment you need to succeed in life. It is your responsibility to look for someone who will love you or at least generously reciprocate your love. If you like to always play it the hard way, you may never find love.
Required	Seek those who naturally love you and don't ever let them go.

Question for Reflection

1. Write down, at least, three (3) qualities you will find in people who value you. (Your answer may include; speak up for you in your absence; enjoy spending time with you; easily renders to help when you are in need, except when you have abused their usefulness, etc.)

    a. ....
    b. ....
    c. ....

14

The Law of Stability

Consistency commands respect.

Falacy
You can get into a relationship and break up at will. You have nothing to lose.

Fact
For every break up, you lose something. Sometimes, something so big that you may never want to relate again.

Basic Truth
Be careful before you get too intimate with a person or group. Check for a person's level of stability before you start relating freely with the person. People who are easily angered, love money, argue over trivial matters, enjoy undue competition, tell lies, are bossy, tribalistic or fanatical may be unstable in relationships.

We must understand, no man is born stable, and educational pursuits do not guarantee stability, either. Growth and stability is a deliberate achievement. You must take the initiative; stability comes with a great deal of personal effort. You must be tactful; listen to people, be patient and respond to them objectively. Avoid destructive attitudes. Seek to give

Required

people all the help they may need—be useful. Over look offences; forgive and forget.

Do these things long enough and people will consider you someone they can count on. Someone they trust enough to listen to, because stability commands respect and makes you a reliable person.

Work on yourself daily, strive to be more understanding and your relationship with people will be more stable.

Question for Reflection

1. Express your feelings about your experience with the loss of a loved one or a broken relationship (with someone you still care about).

   ....
   ....
   ....
   ....
   ....
   ....

2. Write down five (5) factors to consider before going into or initiating a new relationship. (Check content for hints)

   a. ....
   b. ....
   c. ....
   d. ....
   e. ....

15

The Law of The Rough Road

There is no easy ride in any relationship.

Falacy	Good relationship is supposed to be without conflict.
Fact	Conflict is inevitable in any relationship. Conflict tests our resolve in a relationship.
Basic Truth	Frankly, we all want a peaceful and an understanding friend. One who condones our excesses and covers the gaps for our weaknesses. True friends may be that good but it does not stop conflict from emerging. There is no perfect relationship.

People are different. Our personal history, nature, ambition, passion and lifestyles differ. A very small difference between us and our friends, teams or spouses is enough to create a huge gap or misunderstanding. You cannot be like someone else and this difference may sometimes create conflict.

However, as human being we are a work in progress towards perfection and maintaining cordial relationship. When you are wrong be humble enough to admit it and apologize, but when your friend is wrong, show understanding, since it is established no man is perfect. You may even forgive him even before he renders any apology. Since conflict is inevitable in every relationship, patience is, therefore, key in achieving peace during rough times and relationship success.

Required

In conflict show understanding; when at an advantage, be merciful and ready to forgive.

Questions for Reflection

1. In every relationship, no matter how good, ... is inevitable.

2. Mention three (3) factors that may lead to conflict in relationship.

   a. ....
   b. ....
   c. ....

3. .... is key in achieving relationship success.

(Check content for the hints)

16

The Law of Symbiosis

Relationship benefits all.

Falacy	If you are too good people will always take advantage of you.
Fact	Whatever good thing you do for people, you do for youself.
Basic Truth	When you are determined to lead a successful life, being good to people must become your lifestyle. We only relate with people by what we share with or give to them but not what we hold back. Anything you hold back from a person for selfish reason, does not impact positively on your relationship with that person. If you hold back too many things from a person, your relationship with that person will suffer harm and die off.

However, it pays to be generous; it pays to relate well with people. For all we give to people are never lost but are investment for our own future gain.

Let me share this testimony of a young man called Tobi. Tobi was already an orphan in his first year in college. He had to go through college without financial support from his parents.

In his fourth and final year in college, it appeared Tobi will not graduate, because his academic and financial needs escalated. Fortunately, Mr. Badmus, who greatly benefited from the generosity of Tobi's mother, paid him a visit. At his departure he handed Tobi some money, without him making any demand. The money was enough to help him complete his registration and clearance, and was able to graduate with his course mates.

Relationship is the shield of the wise. Fools walk alone and suffer harm.

Required

Support people when they need help and appreciate generously when people show you kindness.

Questions for Reflection

1. .... must be a lifestyle when you are determined to live a successful life.

2. We relate with people by what we ....

3. State why it pays to relate well with people.

....
....
....

4. "Relationship is the shield of the wise." Those who reject this truth are ....
   ....

   (Check content for the hints)

17

The Law of Relative Balance

People relate with you in the way you position yourself to relate with them.

Falacy	People are supposed to relate with you in the same manner.
Fact	People relate with you, in the manner you present yourself to them.
Basic Truth	We do not relate with people in the same way, but in the manner in which they present themselves to us. It, therefore, follows that if you present yourself in a different way to the same person, he will start relating with you differently.

People have some basic assumptions about you. Your actions, interactions and reactions validate or annul such assumptions. On 22nd January, 1916, the Chicago Tribune published an article which libeled Henry Ford as the enemy of the state and a man incapable of thought as to know the "ignominy of his performance".

Does this article have an effect on the

people? Yes, it does strongly; even though the truth was not authenticated, some people took it badly because Ford was a public figure. One Dr. J. M. Postle, after reading the attitude of Henry Ford as presented by the Tribune, took his Ford car to the blacksmith shop and pounded every trace of the name of Ford off his car.

On 23rd June, 1916, the Unity Press wrote an article in the defense of Ford. However, the attack on Ford's personality was so strong that it would require much more than a single article to redeem his public image. Ford sued the Chicago Tribune but it took three years before the case would receive a hearing and the court proceedings took more than two months.

In one of the court's proceedings the Tribune lawyer, Stevenson Elliot, cross-examined Ford to prove their claim was true. Ford was asked a range of questions, ranging from "Who was Benedict Arnold?" through to "How many soldiers did the British send over to America to put down the Rebellion of 1776?" His answers show complete ignorance of public knowledge.

Henry Ford's response as the questions get more and more outrageous and irritating demonstrated his ability to regroup. He pointed his finger at the lawyer who asked the questions, and spoke in a manner that floored the court and ended the hearing in an instant. "If I should really want to answer the foolish question you have just asked, or any of the other questions you have been asking me, let me remind you that I have a row of electric push-buttons on my desk, and by pushing the right button, I can summon to my aid men who can answer any question I desire to ask concerning the business to which I am devoting most of my efforts. Now, will you kindly tell me, why I should clutter up my mind with general knowledge, for the purpose of being able to answer questions, when I have men around me who can supply any knowledge I require?"

With this response he stopped the fun of the lawyer and silenced every one laughing him to scorn. There was silence in the court. Ford's response knocked the questioner cold and confused many of the jury.

That is the law of the relative balance in operation. When Henry Ford's responses lacked substance, the lawyer took the driver's seat, but when he replied soundly, gravity shifted in his favour. People relate with you as you are; when you change, you challenge them to relate with you differently.

Required

Present yourself to any man, in the manner you want the person to relate with you, it does not matter how you had related with him previously. It is never too late to change people's opinion of you.

Questions for Reflection

1. In what manner do we relate with people?

   ....
   ....
   ....

2. State what a man can do to change the way people relate with him.

   ....
   ....
   ....

3. You must present yourself to people in the manner in which you want them to ....

   (Check content for the hints)

18

The Law of the Coloured Glass

Love beautifies the way we see life.

Falacy	The days of love are long gone.
Fact	**Love colours the way we see people and challenges us to make the sacrifices that improves our team and partners.**
Basic Truth	You must have heard the saying that, "Love can never fail". This is very correct, because love colours the way we see people. When we are living the life of love, it challenges us to make sacrifices that improve our teams or partners. Love helps us to see the good in people and look beyond what we can get from them. It helps us to believe our little efforts are making a big difference in the life of someone. The life of Apostle Paul and Mother Teresa, whose love for people create a wave of influence that outlasted their existence, made it clear that a life of love is a high quality life. Love is indeed timeless. Live it and your life along with that of those around you, will be more beautiful.

| Required | Always make effort to put smiles on other people's face. |

Questions for Reflection

1. .... beautifies the way we see life.

2. Love helps us to belief our little effort is..

3. Why is love said to be "timeless"?

   ....
   ....
   (Check content for the hints)

19

The Law of Influence

Change is always under influence.

Falacy

We can get along fine with people without them changing us.

Fact

We are a product of our environment. This environment is made up of two categories of people: those with whom we spend most of our time and those we value.

Basic Truth

Unfortunately, when it comes to environmental influences, the strongest influence is often the negative. It is easier to carry on with a negative attitude than to adjust to positive.

When I was a boy, a certain woman brought her brother who she believed was a strong Christian to come live with them. She expected her brother to serve as a source of strong positive influence to her husband, who was a drunkard. It happened that her husband was a stronger influence than her brother. Consequently, the brother gave in to alcoholism and his life went down the hill worse than that of her husband. The brother eventually died of alcoholism.

Do not joke with the company of people with negative attitudes. They can turn you into what you do not want to be, and make everything good about you to become a thing of the past. The Bible warns, "Evil communication corrupts good manners". When you keep hanging around people with bad attitude, you are preparing yourself for a bad change. Not even Prophet Isaiah, in the Bible, was spared (Isaiah 6:5).

However, we have influence over those who hold us in high esteem. Those who value you are easily influenced by your actions. When you are in trouble, it is not wise to seek out new people for help but first consider people who are concerned about our wellbeing. Again, when you want to start up a new career, people who value you will give the platform to start and succeed. Therefore, relationship increases people's influence. The more you connect and relate with people the greater your ability to make them do things for you.

Required

Take a look around you. Evaluate the people whom you are constantly in contact with and make the decision to distant yourself from those who do not uplift your spirit, encourage you to be a better person or desire to mentor you to grow into your full potential.

Questions for Reflection

1. Mention two (2) people who can easily influence you.

    a. ....
    b. ....

2. List two (2) people you must avoid in life.

    a. ....
    b. ....

3. Mention three (3) positive influences you need in life for a desired change.

    a. ....
    b. ....
    c. ....
    (Check content for the hints)

20

The Law of Investment

When we love we invest; when we invest we tend to love.

Falacy	What we invest does not show how much we care.
Fact	"For where your treasure is, there will your heart be also" (Matthew 6:21, King James Version).
Basic Truth	Relationship is the greatest investment any man can ever have. This is because, it yields the greatest returns—Loyalty. When you continue to invest your time, money and emotions in relationship, eventually it (investing in relationship) becomes a part of you; you will be pleasantly shocked by what people will be willing to do for you. I was in church one day, the woman sitting next to me needed a pen, so I offered her mine and asked her not to bother returning it. She gave me something bigger, because she was moved by my willingness to invest. Investing in people may not always work that way, but it always yields the greatest returns.

Investing in people does not only affect how much they love us but it also increases our affection for them. The more you invest in a person the more you tend to love that person. I have heard people say that they have never fallen in love before. This is because they have not cultivated the habit of investing in people and relationship.

Why do you think most parents have great love for their children? They have invested so much in the relationship with their children. Investing in people triggers our emotional attachment towards them. The more you invest in a relationship, the more you become emotionally attached. To control your emotion towards a person, control your investment in the relationship with that person—To sever a relationship, stop investing in the relationship; so also, to improve relationship, increase your investment in that relationship.

When we are addicted to investing in people, where ever we turn, we will find people willing to follow us, or at least walk with us. Investing in people and relationship commands people's loyalty.

Note the following when you invest in a relationship:

- Investing in a relationship must be deliberate; not by mistake.
- Investing in a relationship must be continuous; do not stop.
- Investing in a relationship must be consistent; make it meaningful.

Required	– Investing in a relationship must be purposeful; have a target. – Investing in a relationship must be affectionate; how you do it matters. – Investing in a relationship must sometimes be sacrificial; it matters most when it hurts. Give your time, words, materials, money and yourself; give whatever it takes to make people you care about get better. Command loyalty!

Questions for Reflection

1. .... is the greatest investment anyone can ever have.

2. Investing in people does not only affect how much they love us, but it also ....

3. Why do you think most parents have great love for their children?

   ....
   ....

4. When we are addicted to investing in people, where ever we turn, we will find people willing to follow us, or at least walk with us. True/False

5. Mention five (5) things you must bear in mind (note) when relating with people.

   a. ....
   b. ....

c. ....
d. ....
e. ....
(Check content for answers)

21

The Law of Authority

God authorized you to love and express it.

Falacy	Only those that are favoured by life have the right to love.
Fact	Everyone can and has the right to love and show it.
Basic Truth	According to the scriptures, "He that loveth not knowth not God for God is love" (1 John 4:8, King James Version). This makes it clear that love is not only in your nature, as it is in God's nature, but that God expects you to express this love. Independent of your personal history, education or family culture, you can feel and express love. Moreover, just as you have the right to love and show it, you also have the right to be loved. Do not cage your destiny, love is your right. Live it!
Required	Remember, you have the right to live the highest quality of life possible—which is love. Dare to love!

Questions for Reflection

1. You are authorized by God to love and express it. True/False.

2. List three (3) factors limiting people from freely expressing love.

   a. ....
   b. ....
   c. ....
   (Check content for the hints)

22

The Law of Identity

Relationship defines people.

Falacy	You do not need people in your life; you just have to be yourself.
Fact	If you do not have people in your life, you cannot tell whether you are bad or good. In fact, it is most likely that you are bad.
Basic Truth	Relationship gives you identity. People are defined by how much they are valued by the members of the group they belong.
	Relationship is of great importance to us. It sometimes gives us reason to win, stand for what we belief and live. We want to know and understand ourselves, and relationship helps in accomplishing that. We are positive identity loving creatures. We want to be a strong force; and may sometimes not accept anything that will make us feel anything less. Actually, we want to feel good about ourselves, and when we find ourselves in the company of those who are not interested in relating with us or who do not value us we feel terrible, because our identity is challenged.

Staying around people, who love or value us, strengthens our identity. It gives us courage to face our fears; it raises our spirits to take risks and helps us to be our very best. Unfortunately, sometimes people who love us may hurt us if we are trailing the wrong path. However, if a person loves or truly values you, he will encourage you to take the right steps and give some incentive to help you achieve this.

Required — **Stay in the company of people who value you and define you positively.**

Questions for Reflection

1. People define themselves by how much they are valued by ....
   ....

2. In what situation is a person's identity said to be challenged?

   ....
   ....

3. Mention one (1) thing which, certainly, strengthens our identity.

   ....
   ....

(Check content for the hints)

23

The Law of Flexibility

No relationship can work if people involved are unwilling to grow.

Falacy	People, who love you, will continue to show you love, no matter what.
Fact	To make people continue to show you love, you must respond creatively in being lovable. Always think of different ways to show or appreciate love.
Basic Truth	You desire a spouse or a good friend, wishing the person will come along and make you a better person, as you often see in movies. Therefore, you package yourself well. Someone comes around because you look attractive. Unfortunately, the attitude is out of place. You nag at every mistake, and expect the person to forgive all your inadequacy simply because you said, "I'm sorry". You are selfish but you expect the person to be selfless—in the name of love. The person gets tired and leaves. This happens with one, then another and then another. You conclude that you would never find love, because it does not exist. That is the situation of many.

To be loved, you must be lovable; demonstrate understanding and flexibility. You must make it easy to be loved. You have to be willing to get better with a relationship; anything that will not help the relationship to grow, has to go if you want the relationship to work. Adopt what is good about the other person and make yourself better for the relationship. Encourage the other person to improve for the sake of the relationship. If they are not willing to, walk away and seek love somewhere else.

The good news is, if you are flexible (that is, growing), you will not only find love, but also good people who will help you succeed in life. However, if you are rigid (that is, unwilling to change or get better), even bad people will not be comfortable around you, because even they are on the lookout for the good guys.

> Required

In the pursuit of successful relationships, we must be willing to learn, and learning cannot be achieved without being flexible. This flexibility helps us to be open to new knowledge and more creative way of showing and reciprocating love.

Questions for Reflection

1. To make people continue to show you love, you must respond

....

2. To find good people who will help you succeed in life, you must

   ....

3. Mention one (1) thing that brings even a good relationship to an end, while the people relating still live.

   ....
   ....
   (Check content for the hints)

24

The Law of Sanity

You cannot be sane if you maintain unhealthy relationship.

Falacy	Hanging around dangerous people will protect me from harm.
Fact	Harmful people are selfish and often hurt people closest to them.
Basic Truth	Keeping relationship with unhealthy or harmful people is unhealthy. More so, not all relationship involving good people are healthy. The following may give rise to unhealthy relationship: • When the person occupying a position that influences the lives of others in an organization is unstable, the relationship within the system will be unhealthy. • When you are not getting along well with someone determined to be intimate with you, even though they appear to be good, the relationship will be unhealthy.

- When it is obvious your partner is a negative or bad person, the result is unhealthy relationship, no matter how hard you try.
- When the person you consider your friend, does not believe in you or your vision, the relationship cannot be healthy.
- When people you count on change for the worse and become unreliable, the relationship will become unhealthy.

All unhealthy relationships affect our psychological being. If you stay too long under the influence of an unhealthy relationship, your sanity will be affected.

Required

Avoid unhealthy relationships.

Questions for Reflection

1. All unhealthy relationships affect our ....

2. Your sanity will be affected if you stay too long under the influence of ....

3. List four (4) instances that may give rise to unhealthy relationship.

   ....
   ....
   ....
   ....

   (Check content for the hints)

25

The Law of Intimacy

People in intimate relationship share and keep secrets.

Falacy It does not take more than ten minutes to know a person.

Fact It may take quite a long time and high level of intimacy to understand and know a person.

Basic Truth People have deep secrets they cannot share with anyone except people intimate with them. Intimacy is not cheap. It comes at a very high price. The prices are time and respect we invest into the relationship with people. Until you pay these prices consistently over time, people are not going to let down their guards.

Sometimes, a man may die with the burden they bear or the treasure at their disposal, because they cannot find someone willing to pay the price for intimacy.

Elisha, the great prophet, carried the anointing transferred to him by his master Elijah, at Elijah's departure, because he paid the price for intimacy. However, Elisha died with the burden of not having anyone willing to be intimate enough to receive the anointing. It was quite unfortunate that Gehazi, the closest person to him, chose the benefits of the anointing over intimate relationship with his master. His greed got the better of him and brought leprosy upon him and his generation.

Required

Give everything to stay close not only to those you value, but also to those who value you.

Questions for Reflection

1. List two (2) prices you must pay to achieve intimacy with a person you value.

   ....
   ....

2. State a condition, in relation to intimacy, when a person will not mind to die with the burden he or she is bearing.

   ....

3. It takes a .... and high level of .... to understand and know a person.

   (Check content for the hints)

26

The Law of the Open Door

Close the door to your past before it consumes or destroys you.

Falacy	Old ways of life and relationship fade away with time.
Fact	**If you keep the door opened to past relationship and ways of life, you are leaving an in-road to the old life, thereby putting your present and future relationship at risk.**
Basic Truth	Most people handle relationship carelessly. Our relationship with people do not always end when we say so, but when there is a mutual agreement or understanding by all parties involved to bring it to an end. Thinking we have autonomy to relate freely, make us end relationship without considering the pains it causes to the other person(s).
	Sometimes people are badly hurt when their feelings are toiled with. When this happens, people dissatisfied try to get even by being vengeful and may seek the slightest opportunity to wreak havoc.
	Moreover, each door we leave open affects

us emotionally. With each door left opened, a person's emotional state is disturbed and with too many doors opened to past relationships, a person may change from good to bad. If these doors stay opened for far too long, everything good about a person might be destroyed.

Imagine how you will feel when someone calls off a good business deal or love relationship—it hurts! Many problems may come from not closing doors to past relationships.

For your own good, it is wise you forgive people who hurt you. However, do not expect people to forgive you without making effort to close the door to a past relationship, appropriately.

The question is; how do I close the door?

Whether it is business or love relationship, the requirement is the same. Allow relationship to linger on for some time, while reducing commitment gradually until the other party reduces his emotional investment. Then you can apologize most sincerely and may also give gifts or a sum of money as compensation. Compensatory business may also help.

He that makes the move to end a relationship closes the door.

Required Kill interest before you walk away. Ensure that every closed door remains shut.

Questions for Reflection

1. People are careless with the way they handle relationship because of the wrong assumption that

   ....

2. List three (3) practical steps to take in order to close the door to past relationship.

   ....
   ....
   ....

   (Check content for hints)

27

The Law of Reconciliation

A once beautiful but battered relationship can be rebuilt.

Falacy	If a person truly loves me, he must be ready to forgive me whether I ask for forgiveness or not—Things always smoothen up themselves.
Fact	When you make a good relationship become sour, do not assume that the relationship will smoothen itself out, reconcile.
Basic Truth	Every relationship that has gone sour can be sweetened again, if one reconciles appropriately. Peter denied Jesus three times but reconciled and was forgiven. The prodigal son returned home after he had squandered his portion of his parent's asset, fell to his father's feet and asked to only be a servant, since he had abused his position as a son. On seeing his sincerity, his father forgave him and restored him, as a son. Judas Iscariot, on the other hand, betrayed Jesus, but failed to reconcile, rather he went and committed suicide.

To reconcile is to put things in order with the aim of recovering or sustaining a relationship.

We are not perfect. We make mistakes in relationships, but we can get back our relationships by making appreciable effort. Yet many people neglect this great opportunity to make their relationship as beautiful as they once were. It is not a bad thing for the person who loves more to make the first move, but it is the responsibility of the one who has done the harm to reconcile. To reconcile, you must forgive yourself, swallow your pride and ask for forgiveness. There is every chance that you will be forgiven and the relationship will be great again, if you ask in humility and sincerity.

Required

If a sour relationship was once beautiful, it can be beautiful again—reconcile.

Questions for Reflection

1. When a person loves you, he or she will always be willing to forgive you whether you do the right thing or not. True/False

2. List three (3) steps involved in reconciliation.

   ....
   ....
   ....
   (Check content for the hints)

28

The Law of Persistence

Love never gives up.

Falacy	Once things are tough, pull out.
Fact	When the hard way becomes the only way, resilience becomes the most required virtue.
Basic Truth	Sometimes things may not go as planned and winning the heart of the people we need may become tough. Then our resilience is tested. How strong our desire is, will be revealed by the extent to which we are persistent. Most things you desire will not come to you until your resolve is tested.

Teju was of age to marry, and she had hopes to marry a man who truly loves her. However, she had six suitors proposing marriage to her at the time. Judging by their actions and words, Teju was convinced that all suitors were serious and determined, this made her confused. To clear her confusion, she sought counsel from the Pastor of her church. The pastor gave her a simple suggestion, "Tell them that you intend to do your Master's Degree and then, your Doctorate before you will be prepared to settle down". She took the advice seriously. Told the six men what the pastor said she should tell them. They all disappeared, and this gave room for the real man to come along later on. Persistence in relationship is a strong demonstration of love.

Your persistence can make any man alter his resolve, whether in business or love relationship. You can make any man change his mind, if you hold out long enough.

> "Saying, There was in a city a judge, which feared not God, neither regarded man: And there was a widow in that city; and she came unto him, saying, Avenge me of mine adversary. And he would not for a while: but afterward he said within himself, Though I fear not God, nor regard man; Yet because this widow troubleth me, I will avenge her, lest by her continual coming she weary me" (Luke 18:2-5, King James Version).

Required

To show your desire is sincere, you must persist.

Questions for Reflection

1. What is the most required virtue when the hard way becomes the only way?

2. You must .... to show your desire is sincere.

3. Recall how persistence has once helped you achieve something you desire. Briefly narrate the story.

   ....
   ....
   ....
   ....

   Apply this principle to your relationship.
   (Check content for hints)

29

The Law of Affinity Between Opposite Sexes

The opposite sex attracts and can easily appeal to a person's emotion.

Falacy We relate in the same way with all sexes.

Fact Relating to the same sex appeals more to our reasoning, but relating to the opposite sex appeals more to our emotions.

Basic Truth Although, it is true that some people prefer dealing with the same sex as themselves, it is easier for the opposite sex to trigger a person's emotion. Some companies have been able to seal more business deals by applying this law. They simply allow the opposite sex to deal with the client.

People have gotten unexpected job offers and gained unimaginable favour simply by appealing to the emotion of the opposite sex. For instance, if a lady tells a man that he is handsome, the man tend to feel good about himself and may even be temporarily thrown off balance. The same thing goes from a man to a lady.

Affinity with the opposite sex also account for why people often do well when they take up a career dominated by the opposite sex.

Three elements play crucial role in affinity with the opposite sex: appearance (neatness), tone of voice and content of words. If the mix is right affinity is sure, but if not the opposite is inevitable.

However, if affinity with the opposite sex is not well managed, it may lead to immoral relationship.

Required

To gain advantage in relationship with the opposite sex, compliment them. Seek to strike the cord of emotion.

Questions for Reflection

1. Mention five (5) good things about your spouse.

   ....
   ....
   ....
   ....
   ....

   (Always let them know you see these things in them. You may also do the same to your good friends or client.)

30

The Law of Emergency

Everyman for himself; God for us all.
—Joy Chia

Falacy   Friends must depend on each other in all situations.

Fact   When a man depends on another in the same emergency situation as himself; catastrophe always compound.

Basic Truth   In an emergency situation the problem is the same but the approach must be individualistic.

John and Rock are good friends working in the same organization. It happened that the organization was downsizing and they were both affected. The issue was an emergency for these friends. Rock knew one of the members of the Board of Trustees who can reverse management decision in his favour. He informed John, his friend, about his decision to see someone who can help him. On hearing this, John caught a glim of hope and intends to seize the opportunity to retain his job and so, he pleaded with his friend that he may go with him.

They both went to see this influential man in his office. He welcomed them both and offer them seat. Rock tabled his problem and entreated that he and his friend be reinstated. In disappointment, the man replied, "If it had been only you that required my help that would have been easy, but now that you are not the only one involved there is nothing I can do about it."

Wisdom did not avail Rock to solve his problem before offering to help his friend. Although, he had influence big enough to solve his problem, he allowed his friend to ruin his chance. It is good to be good, but when in an emergency situation, wisdom require that you look out for yourself before attempting to help another.

Required

In an emergency, everyone affected must depend on their individual influence to solve their problems. If you have none, depend on God—for there is no influence bigger than God.

Questions for Reflection

1. Have you ever been in an emergency situation before? Yes/No.

2. If you are in an emergency situation and you have no one to turn to or anyone with an influence big enough to solve your problem, who can you turn to

....

(Check content for hints)

31

The Law of the Boundary

Knowing your place, with God and men, relating within its confinement and navigating to the greatest height of acceptability, is wisdom.

Falacy

With intimate friends, there are no boundaries.

Fact

Boundaries exist and are the distinguishing elements in relationship. Relating within acceptable boundaries show respect for one another.

Basic Truth

In every relationship there are boundaries. People have dos and don'ts. The dos of a person are what he expects from others – what is acceptable by him – and the don'ts are boundaries that must not be crossed. A person's ability to adjust his boundaries and accommodate different people from different walks of life at various levels, allows him to assume certain social niche, at the same time. The way a man relates with one person, differs from the way he relates with another. These relationships can range from relating as an employee, with another a pastor, with another a son, with another a brother, with another a friend, with another a husband and with another a father. The man occupies different places in the lives of these people and he is required to play different role and relate differently with each of them. If he acts contrary to what is expected of him, he has crossed the line.

When we cross the line too often, we lose the respect people have for us. If you learn to relate within defined or acceptable boundaries people will hold you in high esteem or at least relate with you respectfully.

A number of factors guide our boundaries with people:

Our Nature

Our personality make-ups are very important in guiding our relationship and determining our boundaries with people. These personalities define the type and number of people with which we can relate or be intimate and the amount of time we like to spend alone.

Our Experience

As we grow older, while relating with people, we discover that we are compatible with fewer and fewer. Usually we expect older people to be wise, but experiences don't always come with age, rather with exposure. These exposures might be personal encounters or experiences of others.

Required

Past Encounter

When you cross a boundary with a person, there may be no going back. If a person doesn't want you to cross a boundary, don't force it; it is possible that someone else has occupied the position you desire or that the person is not psychologically prepared to open up new relationships.

In addition, there are people who consider themselves too good to be intimate with you; you will do yourself good to avoid them, because they will always make effort to deflate yourself-confidence.

On the whole, consider this:-

- Everyman has his place,
- Everyman must know his place,
- Everyman must stay in his place,
- Everyman has to pay a higher price to be qualified for a higher place,
- It is your responsibility to define and occupy your place per time.

Always define your boundary with people.

Questions for Reflection

1. List five of your don'ts

   ....
   ....
   ....
   ....
   ....

   When you relate with people remember they
   have their don'ts. Please, respect that.

32

The Law of Perpetuity

Excessive attachment always ends in pains.

Falacy	If he is mine, he will always be mine.
Fact	No mortal being will last forever, not even time which defines mortality.
Basic Truth	When you share mutual love or respect with another person, you want that relationship to last forever. Unfortunately, no mortal relationship will last forever.

Since nothing lasts forever, here are my advices on matters of relationship:

- **Don't wait till tomorrow:** If you love someone, express your love now. If you intend to give a gift, give it now. If you intend to render help, do it now even with your limited resources. If you want to spend time with the person(s) you love, do your best to make it happen as soon as possible (possibly make the visit right away). Waiting till tomorrow may just ruin that golden opportunity to be happy or strengthen your relationship.

- **Enjoy the moment:** Give your heart and complete commitment to those you value. Live the day as if you have no access to another. In that way, when you are separated, for whatever reason, the cherished moment will be of great comfort, because you held nothing back.
- **Create events and activities with lasting effects:** When you share moments with those you cherished, do things that create lasting memories. Take time out to go to beautiful places, take snap shots and keep the pictures. Seek out opportunities to render valuable assistance and support. Make yourself available and valuable.
- **Accept reality:** Nothing lasts forever. Be ready to let go when the time is up. Don't stop your daughter or son from getting married. Don't resist your friend from going to college because you dread separation. Don't stop the people you value from seizing opportunity that will change their lives forever.

More often than not, separation offers some blessings, in that it can lead us to a beautiful path. It gives us the chance to progress to the next phase of our lives. So when the people you value are gone, be open to new relationship. Make new friends and acquaintances, for

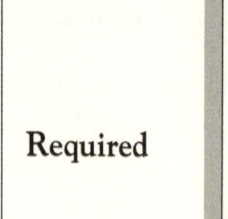

Required

it is a new phase of your life, providing you with the chance to grow stronger and wiser.

Always remember this: - You own no man and no man owns you. All souls belong to God.

Questions for Reflection

1. Since no mortal relationship will lasts forever, list at least four factors that must guide your every relationship.

   ....
   ....
   ....
   ....

   (Check content for hints)

33

The Law of Integrity

You cannot build a solid relationship on a faulty foundation.

Falacy	If you cannot tell lies, people won't love you.
Fact	Every relationship will be tested; only a true relationship will stand.
Basic Truth	We sometimes weaken our relationship with those we love by telling what we consider to be, "white lies". These lies seem harmless because, we mean well for those we love or we intend to cover our flaws in order to keep close to us those we value, but we have no control over their consequences.

Telling lies to those we love does not strengthen the relationship for two reasons. The first is that you lie to those you love for selfish reasons. A lie protects self not the relationship, and as such weakens the relationship. Love rejoices in the truth but not in falsehood. Isaac lied to protect himself from being killed, even though the lie appeared necessary, it could have cost him his marriage (Genesis 26:7-10).

Required

Secondly, you may lie to those you love to cover your flaws. This is often as a result of low self-esteem. When you want to be blameless, outstanding or appear perfect but fail to make corresponding effort to invest in yourself in order to grow up to such height. People who are attracted by this false personality get to know the truth when they get close and discover everything is a lie. These lies often hurt the person you love deeply and cause immediate termination of relationship.

Some people lie about their job to appear more important. They despise their little beginning in order to impress people. Some lie about their status in order to be accepted. Some black people get their skin toned to look like whites. In the end, they lose what is most important about them, their uniqueness or originality and becomes fake. All forms of falsehood are lack of integrity. Falsehood saps your inner strength; you will be nothing more than a surface personality and makes your relationship with people superficial.

There is no future for relationships built on falsehood—uphold your integrity.

Questions for Reflection

1. There is no future for ....

2. Mention two (2) key reasons people tell lies.

   ....
   ....
   (Check content for the hints)

34

The Law of Legacy

You will be long remembered by what you handover to other generations.

Falacy — Once you are good and kind, many generations will remember you.

Fact — Whether good or bad, just or wicked, you will be forgotten as soon as the evidence of your existence is gone. Only your legacy will stand and live beyond generations.

Basic Truth — The people you have read about and all the stories of the great men you have ever heard are not the only most impactful people that ever lived, but the people who built an enduring legacy.

How were these people able to build a lasting legacy? They excelled at a field, handed a furnished structure to their protégés or family and put in place a system to ensure continuity of what they have built. Men and women who built lasting legacy first built up the idea and then the people, unified the people by common goals and motivate them by teaching them productive activities that will perpetuate the legacy as well as profit the person(s). Productive and profitable activities set men on fire.

Jesus is a perfect example of a person who built a lasting legacy. He first came with the ministry, commission twelve people, whom He called Apostles. These men knew Him, and understood what He stood for and represented. He invested in them individually.

He guided and sharpened the perspective of His Apostles. For instance, when they rejoiced that demons bow to the name of Jesus, he told them that they should rather rejoice that their names were written in the Book of Life.

After Jesus built his disciples, he united them. It is easy for a man to lose focus, but a group of people with common goals often inspire one another to stay on course.

Jesus sets his disciples on fire by guiding them through productive activities. He taught them to pray, depend on the Holy Spirit, share the Holy Communion, fellowship together, look out for one another and do several other productive activities, which are necessary to keep their faith alive.

Jesus ensured that his activities were documented for generations to come. He had us in mind when he did these. Written documents are more lasting legacy than spoken words. We never saw Jesus or any of His disciples but we got His messages, because they were written (John 20:31).

Required   **To be long remembered build a lasting legacy.**

Questions for Reflection

1. People are remembered because they ....

2. List five (5) steps Jesus took to build a lasting legacy.

   ....
   ....
   ....
   ....
   ....

   (Check content for hints)

35

The Law of Dignity

Honour is the pillar of marriage.

Falacy

If my spouse behaves well, then I will also behave well.

Fact

Marriage is a high-risk venture. There is every chance that it will not work if you solely depend on your spouse's honour.

Basic Truth

The success of any marriage depends on the honour of both parties involved; not only on the honour of either of them. This is why the marriage vow reads:

> ...for better for worse, in sickness and in health, till death do us part.

It is, therefore, obvious that any side of the coin is possible; things may get better or worse. If you depend on your spouse's honour only, your marriage will have more problems than it ordinarily would. You will give too much credence to frivolities and negative thoughts, which have the capacity to overwhelm you. And when these things happen, you will spend a lot of time and energy fighting to save your marriage or may give up and file for divorce.

The wife of Job left Job when he was very sick. She thought all would always be well, because Job was a godly man. But things did not turn out the way she expected. She asked Job to curse God and die. She walked out on her marriage and relationship with Job, when he needed her support the most. Honour makes you stick to your spouse, no matter the challenge. It validates your marriage. For without honour, marriage is hopeless.

Relationship has aura of dignity when the people involved uphold their individual honour.

Required

Always keep to your promises and uphold your vows; they dignify your relationship.

Questions for Reflection

1. On whose honour should your marriage depend?

   ....

2. .... validates your marriage.

3. State one (1) reason many marriages are not working today.

   ....

(Check content for the hints)

36

The Law of Compatibility

Intimacy unveils our weaknesses.

Falacy	We can't be intimate, if we are not compatible.
Fact	Our distinct differences and non-compatibility always unearth what is lacking in our spouses.
Basic Truth	Non-compatibility is a normal phenomenon in very intimate relationships. One of such relationship is marriage. Marriages only work when people relate with understanding and put their differences aside—change for the sake of the marriage in order to build a good home.

People start having problems in their marriages when intimacy uncovers their weaknesses and that of their partners'. The marriage relationship continuum moves from intimacy through non-compatibility to compatibility. If people are willing to make positive changes, their marriage relationship moves from non-compatibility to compatibility, and then forging of a strong family bond. But, if people are unwilling to cross the hurdle of non-compatibility the relationship get sour, issues linger on until it finally collapses.

Everyone in a marriage relationship will at one time or another has to cross the hurdle of non-compatibility, if they are to forge a strong family bond.

The Marriage Continuum

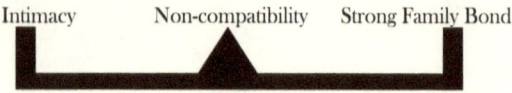

Reasons We Must Overcome Non-compatibility in Our Marriages

- **The society depends on the family:** The family plays a very big role in societal building. Parents must invest quality time in their children. Tell your children, your success stories and failures; share with them principles you have learnt from life. If you invest correctly and adequately your time in your children, individually and collectively, they will give you peace and you will provide the society valuable individuals capable of provoking and sustaining positive societal changes.

   The problem is, we love our children but we don't make the effort to overcome the non-compatibility that exist between us and our spouses, which robs us of the joy and inner peace required to impact positively on our children. The consequences are broken homes and destroyed destinies. If parents fail to overcome non-compatibility, their children will suffer setbacks in life or completely ruined destinies.

- **Our spouse and children are a great source of joy:** There is no better group with whom to spend wonderful moments other than our families. If we overcome the challenge of non-compatibility, we will build good homes that will be a source of great joy and inspiration, invariably the place to be.
- **Our families are our most reliable friends:** Most times, it is easier to get help from a family member than other people. If parents develop love at home, every member of the family becomes a reliable ally; someone that can be called upon in times of need. "A friend loves at all times, and a brother is born to share trouble." (Proverbs 17:17, God's Word Translation).

How to Overcome Non-compatibility in Marriage

- **Sacrifice:** One of the blessings of non-compatibility is that sacrifices are obvious. You and your spouse differ in many things like types of food you enjoy, activities you like to participate in, certain values, language, culture and many more. There is definitely something you like that your spouse doesn't like. So, if he or she goes out of her way to give you that thing special to you, respond in like manner —don't just say thank you, give something special in return.

- **Reward positive action:** You may have been seriously offended or deeply wounded but having a loving family is worth more than any pain you can ever bear. You may not get excited over a simple positive act from your spouse but for the sake of building your home, you have to respond positively. Nothing makes life more colourful than a loving family.
- **Be selfless:** According to John C. Maxwell, the root cause of bad attitude is selfishness. Selfishness places self ahead of others. It makes you desire happiness even if it will bring sorrow to another. There is hardly a home that can survive in a hostile environment controlled by selfishness. Spouses must do everything possible to avoid appearing selfish at any time.
- **Be patient:** We are human; we make mistakes, and therefore not perfect, and we are never going to be perfect. We must be ready to forgive and be patient with one and another, especially that someone committed to spending and investing their time in us. Always be kind with words— Show understanding, and remember, a gentle tongue can break the bone.
- **Give irresistible gifts:** There is a part of us that is childish. We can never grow out of certain habits or hobbies; hence there are certain gifts we never resist. It may be jewelries, parties, craving for attention, (men) teaming up with your spouse to do house chores, going out together to watch movies and so on. Learn how to trigger the

childish nature in your spouse and spice up your relationship.

- **Embrace the larger picture:** The world does not revolve around you. Sociologists tell us the most introverted of people will influence 10,000 others in an average lifetime. Think of the effect of your actions on your spouse and children and what type of influence they will have on people as a result of what you invest in your family.

- **Seek help:** When your marriage relationship is troubled you may need to seek the help of a marriage counselor. Your pastor, parents or a friend gifted with the ability to give sound counsel, can suffice in the absence of a counsellor.

- **Eliminate alternative(s):** Nothing fuels non-compatibility in marriage like alternatives. As long as you are seeing someone else or have eyes for someone other than your spouse, your marriage will not receive the attention and resources it deserves. Most conflicts between spouses arise when a person compares his or her spouse with another. If you really want the most peaceful life and home, you must take your eyes off other people, except your spouse. Be a one-man or one-woman person. Be determined to live your life with only your spouse and children.

- **Pray always:** Mr. and Mrs. Oliver's marriage had been going through turbulent times and something had to be done quickly to prevent it from hitting the rock.

By a striking fortune, she stumbled across a story of a woman, who non-compatibility got the better of her marriage. Who, being short of options combated it in prayer. After about thirty days of consistent prayers, things changed and peace was restored to her home. Her faith was triggered by this testimony; she tendered her case before God in prayer and peace was restored in her home. If you have tried all and nothing worked, try this and you will see result. Demonstrating faith through prayer and fasting to God may be all you need to get back your life and marriage. As long as you are a praying family, you will be a united family. If God is in charge of your home, peace is a sure factor.

If other people's marriages are working yours can also work. You must be determined to overcome non-compatibility and forge a strong family bond.

Questions for Reflection

1. When do people start having problems in their marriages?

   ....

2. What hurdle must be crossed in order to forge a strong family bond in marriages?

   ....

   (Check content for hints)

37

The Law of Consistency

The society can change, but the values that hold a family together remains the same.

Falacy	What once was, no longer is, even for the family.
Fact	Family values can never change—they are ageless.
Basic Truth	In the society, leaders can say one thing and do the direct opposite. Those who want to be good will be good. In the family it is not so. Parents must say and do the right things. Their words and deeds must be in synchrony. This is because their words and acts determine, largely, what children learn, their believe system and become in life. Parents must model love, hard work, truthfulness, courage (actions showing hope), integrity and faith in God. They must stand for what they believe, not only for their own good but also for the good of their children. Parents are not to just watch their children succeed, but also guide

and push them to. They must encourage what they want to see in their children, in words and deeds.

When parents choose to be inconsistent, the family will be in disarray. When there are clear disparities between what parents say and do, the family will be divided. Each member of the family will seek his own value and patterns from an already decayed societal system.

When the family lays the foundation for strong and lasting relationship life, it infuses into the society people who can make positive fundamental changes. If the family fails to build up its members, the society is hopeless.

Required

"Train up a child in the way he should go: and when he is old, he will not depart from it" (Proverbs 22:6, King James Version).

Questions for Reflection

1. Family values are ....

2. List five (5) family values.

   ....
   ....
   ....
   ....
   ....

   (Check content for hints)

38

Operating and Suspending Natural Laws

Obeying or breaking natural laws attract consequences that cannot be manipulated.

The laws of relationship are natural laws; they are not put in place by man. So also are the consequences; they cannot be manipulated by man. Laws exist in nature. Almost every existing law can be suspended by the operation of another law. In reality the law is not broken, but only temporarily suspended by putting in operation another law. However, if you suspend a law for far too long by the excessive operation of another law, the law in operation loses its effect on the law suspended and the law suspended is broken. Airplanes, for instance, may suspend the law of gravity by operating the law of aerodynamics, but this suspension is temporary, has it cannot stay air-borne forever without responding to the law of gravity, at some point in time. One of the dangers of breaking natural laws is that, they are followed by natural penalties, which may not seem immediately apparent until the situation is almost irredeemable. We must therefore understand and operate various laws, giving them their due places.

Breaking the Laws of Relationship have its Consequences

Moses (Exodus 2-3; Exodus 32:12-14; Deutronomy 1:13-14; Numbers 20:8-12)

Moses, one of the greatest leaders that ever lived, continuously suspends the law of clarity by operating the law of common language. The bible describes him has the meekest man on earth, in his days. Moses always finds a common ground with his people and was able to lead them all the way out of Egypt. However, Moses' suspension of the law clarity for far too long took its toll on him—he always waits until he can no longer bear things and then explode angrily—it cost him the Promised Land.

Lot (Genesis 12:4-5, 18:32-33; 19:12, 13, 24, 25 & 26)

Lot, Abraham's nephew, suspended the law of influence by operating the law of relative balance for far too long. The result is disastrous. He was certainly the most God fearing man in Sodom and Gomorrah. When the land experienced God's wrath due to the great height of wickedness of the people of the land, his righteousness only spared him, but he lost everything he had, even the most special person to him—his wife.

Samson (Judges 16)

Samson, like lot, took for granted the law of influence, compensating himself for his good work with Delilah, a harlot and arch enemy. Operating the law of sacrifice and responsibility towards his people, makes him felt so secured as to allow any kind of person into his life without him being influenced. Samson thought himself untouchable. But he was wrong; he had to pay with his life. You must choose with care the people around you. Do not cleave to or hang around people, who can add no value to you—people who don't add value to you, will make you less valuable.

We all have excessively suspended different laws and have carelessly broken others. We have suffered the consequences of our actions, and bore the pains of things and opportunities we have lost that can never be regained. It is time to start relating right and to start building lasting relationships and achieving worthwhile goals.

39

Remember the Golden Rule

Do unto others what you expect them to do unto you.

> "Therefore all things whatsoever ye would that men should do to you, do ye even so to them: for this is the law and the prophets." (Matthew 7:12, KJV).

Abraham Lincoln was a man from a humble background but with a great vision. One day, he walked 40 miles to listen to one of the best lawyers, known for his great oratory, who was to defend a client charged with murder. When the lawyer was done and on his way out, Lincoln met the lawyer, stretched out his hand and said, "I walked forty miles to hear you, and if I were to do it over, I would walk a hundred". Unfortunately for Lincoln, the man was too arrogant to consider him someone deserving his attention—the lawyer walked out on Lincoln without speaking a word.

When Lincoln became the president of the United States, this same great lawyer came to petition the president on behalf of a man condemned to death. Lincoln listened to what the lawyer had to say, after which he reminded the lawyer of his unwelcoming act at their first meeting before he signed the pardon. The lawyer was broken that he could only mutter a brief apology.

You must do unto others what you want others to do unto you. The Lawyer looked down on young Lincoln, but he had no power over the future. When Lincoln had the power to repay the Lawyer, he chose to forgive. The president, Abraham Lincoln, seized the opportunity to do things right. He simply did what he expected the lawyer to do to him, had roles been switched.

Be to others how you expect them to be in relating with you and do to them what you will expect them to do to you.

There are, at least, five ways you want others to treat you:

- You want others to encourage you;
- You want others to appreciate you;
- You want others to forgive you;
- You want others to listen to you;
- You want others to be patient and make the effort to understand you.

Go and do likewise.

Strive to apply the golden rule to your relationship and in the end, you will be satisfied that you led a fulfilled life and like Jesus, you can take a deep breath and say, "It is finished", or like Apostle Paul, "I have fought a good fight…"

> *"If you really keep the royal law stated in Scripture, "Love your neighbor as yourself," you are doing well."* (James 2:8, King James Version).

About the Author

An educationist, theologian, and most importantly, good student of relationship, Eric O. Enejoh is endowed with the unique ability to equip people and help them find their places in life. He is based in Nigeria with his wife, Favour, and two children.

www.ingramcontent.com/pod-product-compliance
Lightning Source LLC
Chambersburg PA
CBHW031924240526
45464CB00022B/788